BUSY HUMAN'S SUMMARY
LIESPOTTING
BY
THE MIGHTY JEWMANBERG
(Summarizing Pamela Meyer)

BUSY HUMAN'S SALES PITCH

You are a busy human. You don't have time to read piles of books, think about the best way to understand them, and then write (possibly) the most awesome notes on the planet. Luckily for you, I don't really have much going on in my life, so here we are.

In this volume, I provide you, my dear reader, with a simple and entertaining summary of *Liespotting: Proven Techniques to Detect Deception* by Pamela Meyer.

This is not any old summary. I've tried hard to summarize this useful work in a very understandable manner, and I've added just enough humor to keep you entertained throughout the journey.

Please note that this summary is for educational aid and entertainment purposes only (I sincerely hope that all of the content is totally true, but I'm mostly just trying to summarize a book that somebody else wrote).

Thanks for reading, you busy human!
The Mighty Jewmanberg

CHAPTER 1: The Deception Epidemic

Deception costs businesses about a trillion bucks per year. *A trillion!* And deception in the workplace manifests in so many forms, and much more frequently than you'd think; you're just not able to spot it... *yet*.

We're fooled regularly, perhaps due to **truth bias**. People, especially Americans, are very trusting. People prefer to trust. In some ways we need to trust each other, and it's also neater and tidier. Even if a speaker is ambiguous, we tend to fill in the missing information in a manner that would maintain his truth integrity, but rather often we are mistaken.

And deception detection has become even more challenging in the modern world. The majority of communication is actually done nonverbally, but how useful is body language when you're talking business over the phone, or even worse, through email? (Indeed, I have found that it is almost impossible to bust someone for using an emoji that does not truly represent his current state of mind.)

As if this weren't hard enough, research shows that people feel less guilt about lying at work than in their personal lives. Not to mention that a strong majority of people have told lies in their search for employment.

Administering polygraphs can be useful in the business world, but they can't accomplish everything, and they're not always feasible. Similarly, handwriting analysis could be useful, but that is limited.

So, what can you do? Can *you* become a human lie detector(-ish), learning to spot the lies that lie within words, voice, facial expressions and body language? Not only will this book help you to spot the "tells" that give liars away, it will provide you with insights into the psychology of lying - on how the minds of liars work.

Let's get to work!

CHAPTER 2: Deception 101 - Who, When, and Why

Even an infant will use deception to get what he wants (don't worry, it's normal), and once he learns to speak, a child will often cover his mouth when telling a lie. An adult liar feels the same urge to cover his mouth, but he subdues it; however, he might still touch his mouth area.

Who lies most?

Men and women are about equally guilty. Men tend to lie to make themselves appear better in various ways, whereas women often lie to protect people's feelings. And in regards to being the victim of lies, women take it harder and suffer more.

It's interesting to note that married people usually lie less to their spouses than do unmarried mates, but they do tell bigger lies.

Extroverts are more comfortable lying, and they lie more often than do introverts.

What kind of lies do we tell, and to whom?

Overall, more than 50% of our lies are self-oriented (for the teller's benefit). About 25% of our lies are other-oriented (designed to protect others). Of course, there are lies that are made to protect/benefit both, the liar and others. People tell more other-oriented lies to women (this would include many cases of women lying to women), and more self-oriented lies to men.

People are significantly more likely to lie to coworkers than to strangers. This might be due to the power struggles that invariably permeate the workplace; honesty can create vulnerability, especially in such an atmosphere.

Why do we lie?

Understanding why people lie can help you to become a better liespotter, so let's examine the impetus behind lies, and the goals of liars. We'll divide motives into two categories, offensive (to gain) and defensive (to protect), and we'll examine the nine basic motivations for lying.

Offensive motives:

To obtain a reward that is not otherwise easily available, such as piles of cash.

To gain advantage over another person or situation, such as a liar who feigns interest in something in order to ask questions and uncover information.

To create a positive impression and win the admiration of others, such as lying on a resume, or inflating sales projections.

To exercise power over others by controlling information, such as withholding information to which another party is entitled.

Defensive motives:

To avoid being punished or to avoid embarrassment (a liar might weigh the immediate repercussions of admitting to the crime versus the greater punishment that he could receive if caught lying about it, and decide that lying is worth the risk).

To protect another person from being punished, such as when taking the blame for someone else.

To protect one's self from the threat of physical or emotional harm.

To get out of an awkward situation, such as lying about already having made plans.

To maintain privacy, such as a top executive who lies about the reason that he is stepping down from his position.

What is a lie?

For our purposes, a lie is anything said or done with intent to deceive another person, unless the listener has been given some form of notice that a falsehood is on the way. So, actors aren't 'lying,' because the audience knows that the story is not real, or at least they *should* know (no offense, pro wrestling fans).

Conversely, a guy who mistakenly *thinks* that he's telling the truth is not considered as 'lying' for our purposes, because if he really believes the falsehood then we shouldn't be able to notice any signs of deception on his part, and liespotting is the main purpose of this book.

CHAPTER 3: Reading the Face

There are many involuntary facial expressions that show up on our faces without being invited, and they are programmed to reflect our true feelings. We often try to hide them with phony facial expressions, or *masks*, that do not reflect our true feelings. But even if we successfully put on a mask, a brief **microexpression** of our true emotions will generally make an appearance. If you can spot a microexpression on a subject's face, that can help you to deduce his true feelings.

Now, let's discuss the seven basic human emotions, and how they present in facial expressions.

Fear: Eyebrows rise up, jaw drops open, lips stretch outward, and the chin pulls back.

Sadness: Corners of the lips pull down, upper eyelids droop, and the result is squint-like.

Disgust: Nose scrunches up, and the cheeks and upper lip rise.

Happiness: In a genuine smile, the corners of the mouth pull up, and crow's-feet crinkling forms around the eyes. The eyes also kind of light up.

Contempt: One lip corner pulls in and back, and the chin sometimes rises (as if the subject is looking down on you).

Surprise: Eyebrows rise up, eyelids widen, and the mouth drops open but remains relaxed (as opposed to the expression of fear, in which the mouth stretches more and becomes taut).

Anger: Eyebrows pull down, and the lips narrow, making it look like the red part of the lips has disappeared.

Nine clues to facial deceit: (Note: I have used the book *Telling Lies* by Dr. Paul Ekman to help elucidate some of these descriptions.)

Microexpressions: As explained, there are many involuntary facial expressions that show up on our faces without being invited, and they are programmed to reflect our true feelings. We often try to hide them with phony facial expressions, or *masks*, that don't reflect our true feelings. But even if we successfully put on a mask, a brief microexpression of our true emotions will generally make an appearance. If you can spot a microexpression, that will help you to deduce that the mask which appears afterward is a facial lie.

With practice, such as by taking quick glances at photos and trying to catch the expressions that are on them, you can improve upon your ability to spot microexpressions.

Squelched expressions: A microexpression is a complete, full-on expression, such as a clear look of distress, which lasts for a small fraction of a second. A *squelched* expression, on the other hand, is *not* a full expression, but it usually lasts *longer*. In a squelched expression the subject feels the undesired expression begin to form, so he kind of catches it in the middle and stops it from reaching completion. Maybe it's an inappropriate time to smile, and he manages to freeze the burgeoning smile, leaving a *partial* smile stuck on his face. Or, he might present a quick squelch and transition into a totally different expression. Either way, the squelched expression usually lasts a little longer than does the micro, and even if you don't catch the specific emotion that was squelched, just by catching the squelch you will know that the subject was trying to mask *something*.

Reliable muscle patterns: Some facial muscles are *reliable facial muscles,* which means that it's very hard to use them voluntarily, therefore they are reliable in their *authenticity*. Dr. Ekman hypothesizes that it's also hard to *inhibit* the reliable muscles from doing their thing when the emotion that they would show is genuine. For example, pulling the corners of your lips downward without moving your chin. This is a great indication of sadness, sorrow or grief, and only about ten percent of those tested were able to make the face deliberately, but when the emotion is genuine it appears automatically on the faces of the general population.

Sadness clues include the inner eyebrows (the portion of the eyebrows that are above the nose) pulling upward accompanied by significant creasing in the forehead. This is hard to fake, and phony sadness should present with less creasing in the forehead.

Genuine fear will present with eyebrows pulled up and together, scrunched toward each other, and very few people can fake that. In genuine fear there should also be a raised upper eyelid and a tensed lower eyelid, but these may drop out if the fearful individual tries to conceal his fear.

Eyebrow raises are often used to add emphasis or to convey disbelief.

Narrowing of the lips (pursing), which means that less of the red part is visible, is a good sign of anger.

Blink rates (and reduced eye contact): (Note: some of this is from the book You Can't Lie to Me, by Janine Driver, with Mariska van Aalst):

There is a myth that liars don't make eye contact, but even truthful people only maintain eye contact part of the time. It's awkward for some people to maintain a lot of eye contact, and in some cultures direct eye contact is considered rude, so there would be a good explanation when a subject from such a culture avoids direct eye contact.

Blink rate is a better indicator of deception, at least to an extent, with liars blinking more often. (However, everyone is different, so only an *increase* in the subject's own blink rate or averting his eyes is especially noteworthy, because some people have shifty eyes even when they're telling the truth. But if these eye behaviors change in response to a specific question, then perhaps that question has, indeed, made him uncomfortable.)

Pupil dilation: The pupils widen in response to arousal, including fear, which is something that a liar would feel.

Tears: Tears are relevant in deception detection, but they aren't always limited to sadness, and they can be faked, so use caution in assessing them.

Asymmetrical expressions: Please note that in this section we are *not* discussing an expression that only appears on *one* side of the face, which Dr. Ekman refers to as a *unilateral* expression. Rather, we are discussing an expression that appears on *both* sides of the face, but it presents *unevenly,* such as when there's a stronger expression of anger on one side of the face and a weaker form of that same expression on the other side of the face. That is an *asymmetrical* expression. Unilateral expressions are generally not important in detecting deceit, but asymmetrical expressions are of interest to us.

Although it was a fierce scientific battle, most investigators now agree with Dr. Ekman's findings that *true* facial expressions rarely present asymmetrically, and asymmetrical facial expressions are a legitimate deception clue. If a smile is asymmetrical, it's probably because the subject is forcing the smile.

In asymmetrical smiles, if the subject is right-handed, then the left side of his face should have the stronger half of the phony, asymmetrical smile; and this detail (the right-left phenomenon) isn't present in the relatively small number of *truthful* asymmetrical smiles.

So, fake smiles are more likely to be asymmetrical, and the stronger half of the phony emotion should present on the non-dominant side. But with true smiles, asymmetry will be rare, and even when it happens it won't specifically fit the non-dominant pattern. Once again, there are exceptions, so don't rely on asymmetry/symmetry all by itself to prove deception or lack thereof.

Timing: If the timing of a facial expression doesn't quite seem to match up in a natural manner with the subject's behavior, it could be because he is faking the emotion.

Duration: Genuine facial expressions generally last only a few seconds, almost never longer than ten.

Intuition: Your gut is the tenth indicator. But always ask yourself if there is another explanation for the subject's behavior and expressions.

Get a baseline reading of the subject's behavior patterns while he is calm, and then look for *changes*. Changes in his own *personal* behavior are better deception clues, but even then, assess if there is an alternative explanation, other than deception, for the changes.

On the other hand, if you sense that something doesn't feel right, you might want to trust your gut and pursue the point by asking more questions.

CHAPTER 4: Reading the Body

Liars tend to spend time rehearsing their words before lying to you, but do they prepare choreography? Not so much. And this is one of the reasons that you can learn so much from body language, which, in general, is a strong reflection of a subject's actual thoughts and feelings.

To make up for his lack of choreography, a liar might try to remain as still as possible when lying, so not to provide us with any deception clues. But that won't fool us, because we will remember that stillness is unnatural, and by doing nothing with his body the subject is actually more likely to be doing *something*: lying.

Take all of that, and add in that the liar will face questions which he doesn't anticipate (later in the book, we will learn which questions to ask), and we should see a liar's body light up with deception clues. Now, let's analyze specific signs of deceptive body language.

(Note: Once again, I have used the book *Telling Lies* by Dr. Paul Ekman to help elucidate some of these descriptions.)

Emblems: There are certain physical expressions with which everyone in a given place is familiar. We all know what *the finger* means. Another example is the *"I don't know/I'm helpless"* two-shouldered shrug, which is generally accompanied with some enhancements. The shrugger will usually turn his palms up, and he might make a horseshoe-shaped mouth gape, and he might also throw in a sideways neck tilt.

Most of the time, these types of well-defined gestures are completely *intentional* and meant to convey the meaning that everyone in that particular region ascribes to that particular physical expression. The emblem theory suggests that an *accidental* version of these expressions hints that the subject is actually feeling what the normal, full movement usually represents. The student really wanted to give her professor the finger, because she felt *that* angry. Similarly, someone who does part of a shrug while pretending to know what he's talking about is, in truth, not confident about what he's saying (or he's lying), or he feels helpless.

11

So, how do we go about spotting these accidental, but very meaningful, emblems? There are two rules: One, accidental emblems will be **partial.** Some examples of the unintended shrug emblem would include a half-shrug, in which the shoulders aren't fully raised; a one-shoulder shrug (or half of a one-shoulder shrug); or simply turning the palms up, which is only a *part* of the normal shrug package. Likewise, the intentional finger gesture usually involves turning up the hand and flipping the bird, whereas the unconscious emblem won't have all that, such as the student who simply had her middle finger extended on her knee.

The second distinction is that when these gestures are performed intentionally they're usually made in the **presentation position.** The aforementioned hand gestures, when done intentionally, will usually be presented with the hands being somewhere between the waist and the neck in terms of height, and with the hands positioned a bit in front of the body. The emblem (which is the unintended version) will not present in the presentation position. The finger on the *knee*, or the turning up of the palms *close* to one's body, or a *half*-shrug are all emblematic of the emblem. All of these could indicate that the subject didn't do a good enough job restraining his body, and you just spotted a clue to how he's really feeling.

Not all liars will present an emblem, but perhaps close to half of them will, and emblems are pretty reliable clues, as far as individual deception clues go. This is because the meanings of the emblems are relatively clear and specific. Plus, since barely anyone routinely uses emblems (without actually feeling what the emblem represents), when you spot an emblem it's pretty safe to assume that what you saw was *unusual* for the subject. So, even without a baseline the emblem is meaningful.

Common American emblems include hand waves *hello* and *goodbye*, the *come-here* beckon, head-nod *yes* and head-shake *no*, balled up fists, etc. You will find approximately sixty emblems in any given culture.

Illustrators: Don't even pretend that emblems and illustrators are the same thing, because they're not. Emblems have a very specific meaning and are kind of like making a statement without using words; where-as, the bodily movements called illustrators - which aren't quite as spe-cific, and are not understood on their own merits - are used to *enhance* something *else* that is being said. I can keep my mouth zipped while shaking my head no, and you'll know what I mean - that's an *emblem*. If while I'm telling you *no*, I also wave my hands frantically to let you know just how much I mean *no*, then I've used an *illustrator*. (Presumably, if I shake my head *no*, which is understandable on its own, and I also wave my hands frantically, then the hands are *illustrating* the head-shake.)

Illustrators are often performed with the hands, but other body parts can illustrate too. The style and amount of illustrators an individual uses has a strong correlation to the accepted norms in the culture from which he's from, but not everyone will follow the norms.

But not everyone is the same - maybe a particular subject always uses many, or few, illustrators - so how can you detect deception from illustrators? Well, you'll still have a clue from the *decrease* of illustrators. If the speaker has proven to use a certain amount of illustrators, and then all of a sudden he's using his hands much less, he might be lying. So, that's a big difference between emblems and illustrators. The *presence* of emblems will often help you to detect deception, whereas a *decrease* in illustrators could do the same.

Bear in mind that illustrators also decrease when a person is having trouble *deciding* what to say. That *could* be because he's trying to think of the right lie or struggling with the lie that he wants to tell, but it could also be that he's nervous or concerned because of whatever stakes are riding on his response and word selection.

Illustrators are also connectable to excitement. If someone is bored or sad he will probably illustrate less. So, someone who is *pretending* to be interested might give himself away by his lack of illustrators.

We've focused mostly on judging the lack of illustrators as a possible sign of *concealment*, in the sense that we're guessing that the subject is trying to hide his fear, anger, or sadness, and we're pointing to his lack of illustrators as evidence of that. But be aware that it's also possible for a subject to *increase* his illustrators in order to create the appearance of *not* being afraid or sad. In such instances of *falsification,* you might notice that his phony illustrators aren't quite timed right with the words that they're supposed to be enhancing; the phony illustrators might show up a little early or a little late.

Mirroring: When people are comfortable being together, they tend to mirror each other's behavior. If one leans in a little, the other will often follow suit. However, if a subject does not mirror your actions (for example, you lean in, and then he leans away), this might be a sign of deception.

Bear in mind that, while some deception clues are strong, most deception clues should not be relied upon unless they appear in **clusters**. If multiple signs of deception pop up from the subject, then that is noteworthy.

Also, keep in mind that most of these clues are simply signs of *stress* or *anxiety*. Liars do tend to get nervous, but so do some truthful people. So, if you can form a **baseline** of how the subject behaves while calm, and then notice changes that occur in his behavior in response to specific questions, it would make the deception clues more meaningful.

CHAPTER 5: Listening to the Words

Let's examine the deception clues that can be found in a subject's speech, and we will begin with his his words. The manner in which a subject arranges or frames his speech - **statement structure** - can be telling, especially when he deviates from his baseline speech patterns in response to a specific question. Here are some generally suspicious statement structures:

Parrot statements: By repeating your question before answering it, the subject could be buying time to think of the best lie.

Dodgeball statements: He responds to your question by asking you a question. He might be digging to find out how much you already know.

Protest statements: The subject might whine about how unfair you're being in accusing him, or how you're wasting everyone's time, you dirty little time-waster!

Too little/too much statements: You would expect a truthful subject to provide the relevant details when he answers your question, and you'd expect him not to add too much else. So, if he avoids discussing pertinent details, or if he blabbers on and on (perhaps in attempt to gloss over the most pertinent, potentially damaging details), that is a deception clue.

Bolstering statements: Liars will often try to convince you that their statements are true by swearing on deities, or enhancing their statements with, "To be honest..." or "To tell you the truth..."

Or they'll use an apologetic "but," such as in, "I know you're going to think I'm making this up, *but* I can talk to dead people during a full moon." Or, "I know this is hard to believe, *but* I'm the guy that forced Pluto to admit that it's not a planet."

Distancing statements: A liar who is trying to hide himself from the conversation might avoid using the word "I," even it forces him to use interesting sentence structure.

Similarly, a liar might avoid saying, "They went to *my* house." Instead, he'll say, "They went to *the* house," leaving a personal pronoun out of the sentence.

Euphemisms: This is another form of distancing. You ask a subject if he *stole*, and he responds with, "I didn't *take* anything." He doesn't even want to talk about *stealing*.

Let's move on to **verbal leaks**.

Slips of the tongue: A slip of the tongue *could* reveal a subject's true thoughts.

Non-contracted denials: Assuming that a subject normally uses contractions ("didn't," "wasn't"), but suddenly switches to a non-contracted denial ("I did not," "I was not") it is a deception clue. An honest person would probably want to get to his denial as quickly as possible by using a contraction, while a liar might choose to use a more formal style of language (perhaps due to hesitation, but it could also be because people who stand on formality are supposedly above committing crimes and lying).

Specific denials: If you asked the subject about *overall* company sales, but he answered specifically about *domestic* sales, that's a deception clue.

Speech disfluencies: An *increase* in the use of partial words, and nonwords such as "ah," and "uhh," as well as other fillers, could indicate deception, especially when they present in response to a question. The subject knows that utter silence is suspicious, but he wants a little more time to think of his lie, so he stalls by using these filler words.

Pronoun inaccuracies or inconsistencies: This is when the subject begins to change his pattern of pronoun usage, by skipping pronouns or by leaving out the word "I." He might be nervous and/or trying to hide himself from the conversation, both of which are deception clues.

Vocal quality is a less reliable indicator, but deception signs include talking in a higher pitch and the voice sounding strained.

Attitude: Liars will tend to be uncooperative. They often feign being offended, only to calm down almost instantly once they feel they've put on enough of a show to fool you.

Story Analysis: The author cites lie-detection expert Avinoam Sapir, who explains that emotions shape our storytelling. A truthful storyteller will often be guided by his emotions. He might begin with emotional highlights, and not necessarily tell the story in chronological order. He'll fill in the rest as he goes along. A fake (probably rehearsed) story is less likely to be shaped by emotions (the speaker didn't actually experience the story, at least not all of it), and is more likely to be presented in perfect chronological order.

Also, storytelling is done in three parts. The *prologue* sets the stage for the main body of the story. Then, there is the *main body*, after which there will often be an *epilogue*, in which the storyteller does kind of a post-game commentary on the story. Truthful people won't spend too much time on the prologue, maybe up to a third of the total storytelling time; but a liar feels safer in the prologue, and he might spend more time there. Also, the liar will gloss over potentially important details in the main body of the story, trying to rush through it. Furthermore, a truthful person will feel the pain of the story, and he'll feel the need to discuss his feelings and the impact that the story had on him, in an epilogue; whereas, a liar will often skip the epilogue altogether.

A reminder: look for clusters of deception in speech and/or voice (which can also be combined with other deception clues to form a hybrid cluster), as a cluster is much more telling than is a single tell.

CHAPTER 6: The BASIC Interview Method

It is a well-known fact that no book on lie detection is ever complete without an acronym. **BASIC** = **B**aseline behavior, **A**sk open-ended questions, **S**tudy the clusters, **I**ntuit the gaps, and **C**onfirm. This is a guide on how to conduct a conversation in a manner that will lead to uncovering the truth. The system is divided into five steps, so let's assess them individually.

STEP #1: Baseline Behavior

Baselining means that you get a sense of the subject's normal behavioral patterns. If you get a sense of how he behaves when he's calm and not lying, it will be easier to recognize the tells that present when he is lying. To accomplish this, create an open setting and make the subject feel comfortable. Build a rapport with him, which will encourage him to open up to you. This is not the time to press him; you want the subject to remain calm. This is an especially critical step in the deception detection process, because people have many personal peculiarities and idiosyncrasies, so without a baseline of how the subject acts while calm the process of catching liars can often devolve into a guessing game.

There are five behaviors that you should examine closely during baselining.

Laugh: What does the subject's normal, genuine laugh sound like?

Voice: How fast, loud, and at what pitch does the subject speak while he is calm?

Posture: How does the subject position his body while calm?

Gestures: How often does he make gestures and fidget?

Reactions: How does the subject's facial expressions and posture change in response to true emotions that he actually feels?

After gauging these elements during the getting-to-know-you, softball part of the interview, it will be easier to notice when the subject deviates from his norm, which will often indicate stress and deception.

Profiling: All of those outward expressions of the subject are important elements of baselining, but you should also get to know who he is, which will provide you with context in the main part of the interview. Peek into his psyche, and see what makes him tick. Where has he been, and where is he headed? What are his motivations? How does he perceive himself? Does he tend to take blame upon himself, or does he blame others; this could help you to assess any rationalizations that he might make to himself about why committing the crime or bad act was justified, and why lying about it is okay (but you should really try to anticipate all of the potential rationalizations *before* interviewing him).

STEP #2: Ask Open-Ended Questions

(Note: I have used the book *You Can't Lie to Me* by Janine Driver with Mariska van Aalst to elucidate the category of open-ended questions.)

After baselining, segue (preferably in a smooth, inconspicuous manner) to the main portion of the interview and ask **open-ended questions**. These are questions that the subject can't answer with a simple "yes" or "no." For example, "What did you do yesterday?" Or, "When was the last time you saw Steve?" Or, "Tell me what happened?" "Okay. Tell me more about that..." In answering these questions, the subject will probably have to commit to all sorts of details, placing himself at specific locations and the like.

All the while, you are looking for deviations from the subject's baseline, which will tell you which questions make him antsy and deserve more attention. You might ask some follow-up questions in a gentle manner, by prefacing those follow-ups in a nice way, such as, **"Maybe I'm wrong here, but..."** and then you'd mention the issue, such as, "Maybe I'm wrong here, but it seems like there's more to the story?" Or, "Maybe I'm wrong here, but it seems like you were happy with losing your job?" And then you shush and wait. Allow him to explain his feelings regarding your respectfully worded inferences.

Even during this stage of the interview/interrogation, you would like to avoid speaking in a manner which would prompt the subject to shut down and stop talking, so keep your language and tone soft.

Propose stories: Unlike what is seen on television dramas, interviews/interrogations tend to be rather quiet. The investigator doesn't get in the face of the subject; rather, he tries to collaborate with him, in a sense. He encourages the subject to work with him to get to the truth, or at least that's how the investigator makes it sound. He will begin to propose stories that are designed to mitigate the subject's guilt, proposing one rationalization after another. Perhaps the subject's boss was wealthy, and the subject deserved to be paid more; that's why the subject stole. And there are times when a man has to stand up and be a man, which could explain why an inmate who'd had his tater tots stolen wound up stabbing another inmate with a spork. All the while, the investigator watches the subject's reactions to get a sense of which proposed story resonated the best.

STEP #3: Study the Clusters

As mentioned, a lonely, single deception clue generally isn't all that valuable, so watch out for *clusters* of deception clues in both verbal and nonverbal tells. Also, look for nonverbals that *contradict* the subject's words, such as when he says "yes," but shakes his head horizontally, which suggests that the truthful response would be "no."

STEP #4: Intuit the Gaps

Watch out for these:

Statement gaps: When the subject's statements disagree with the facts.

Logical gaps: When the subject's statements don't make sense in context.

Behavior gaps: When the subject claims that he behaved in a manner which is inconsistent with whom you know him to be.

Emotion gaps: For example, when a subject professes to feel excited, but his facial expressions and/or body language aren't on board with that story.

Don't ignore your gut: Even if you don't spot a clear sign of any of the four gaps, if you have a bad feeling, then there probably is reason to be suspicious, so go with your gut and err on the side of caution to a reasonable degree.

STEP #5: Confirm

Ask questions that can help you to confirm (not necessarily to a definitive degree) your hunches. Here are examples (and I've elucidated some of them with help from *You Can't Lie to Me* by Janine Driver w/ Mariska van Aalst and *Spy the Lie* by Philip Houston and friends):

Ask the **same question** in three different ways ("How old are you?" "In which year were you born?" "When did you graduate high school?"), which could throw the subject for a loop. He'll wonder what's going on, and that will increase the pressure.

Ask the subject **how he feels** about being interrogated. An innocent person might simply be angry, while a guilty subject might think how to respond and then display mixed emotions.

Punishment question: "What do you think should happen to the person who did this?" This is a routine interview/interrogation question. An innocent person would probably recommend a relatively harsh sentence, but what would a guilty person say, considering that he would essentially be sentencing himself (in theory)? Well, if he's shrewd and wants to convince us of his innocence, then he might answer as would an innocent, by suggesting a relatively harsh sentence. Therefore, we can't really glean any strong insights when a subject suggests a relatively harsh sentence, because he could either be innocent or trying to act innocent (or even trying to ingratiate himself with law enforcement by taking a tough stance on crime).

However, how many explanations are there for a subject who responds by suggesting an especially *light* punishment? That's a red flag, and he might be trying to negotiate his potential sentence, just in case he'll get caught. Perhaps especially so when a subject replies, "I would not want jail time." Not only is he talking about a crime that warrants jail time, but it sounds like his brain nudged him to frame the response in personal terms, "*I* would not want jail time." He could have said "*There* shouldn't be jail time," or "*He* shouldn't get jail time," or even "I would not *give him* jail time." So, his response indicates that his mind might be focused on *his* potential jail time (because he's guilty and worried about being caught), which he does not want.

You ask, **"Who could have stolen it?"** A truthful person might respond, "Any of us could have taken it." But a liar will often name other suspects but exclude himself.

Tell the story backward: Ask a subject to do it. Liars usually fail.

Ask the subject to speculate about the **motivations** of the unidentified person who actually did the crime or act. An innocent party is more likely to engage in a normal discussion about it, while a guilty party could either tell an odd tale (perhaps because he's trying to distance the tale from the true story, so as not to give away hints), or he'll be too afraid to even engage in the hypothetical discussion.

Ask a **presumptive question**, which could begin like, "When you and Bob were at the warehouse..." An innocent party might correct you and say that he was alone. But the guilty party has to worry that you have already figured out that Bob was with him, so he might not deny it (thereby confirming it for you).

"How do you think the investigation will turn out?" An innocent party might state unequivocally that he will be exonerated, while a guilty party might hedge and say something like, "I *hope* it will clear me"

Present **two options** of what might have happened, both of which imply guilt on the subject's part, but with different details or two different rationalizations. Then, see if he accepts one version of the story, or how much he corrects you.

A warning: The subject has just told you that he's never driven above the speed limit. Do not follow up with, "Really? You've *never* driven over the speed limit?!" That is the *exact* same question, and once the subject has committed to his response to that exact question, his **psychological entrenchment** will probably only become stronger if you repeat the same question, and he's forced to give you the same answer. Use finesse, and hit the question from a different angle.

CHAPTER 7: Liespotting for High Stakes

High stakes **negotiations** increase the incentive to lie, and people do lie more often when the stakes are raised. Some feel that lying is an accepted part of negotiation, so they don't feel guilty about it, and research indicates that negotiators will behave more honestly when directly informed that they are expected to tell the truth during the negotiation.

Lies of omission are rampant in negotiations. Negotiators will leave out important information, which is easier than falsifying information. Lies of omission are easier in the sense that the liar doesn't have to be very creative. He doesn't have to cook up something false, he just needs to leave out something true.

Additionally, once the liar presents a falsification, he will need to remember the work of fiction which he has created and passed on to his mark, which can be challenging. Omission is easier in this sense, as well.

Omission is also easier for the liar to justify if he gets caught. He can claim that it was an oversight, or that he meant to share the information with you later.

Some negotiators might rationalize their lies by telling themselves that since bluffing (such as in regards to a bottom line - "And that's my *final* offer!") is an accepted part of negotiations, even though bluffing *is* lying, it must be that all bets are off, and other lies are fine too; however, in addition to the moral issues, many of these negotiators end up lying in ways that are actually *illegal*, and their dishonesty might also hurt them financially in the long run.

The author adds some notes on **women in negotiation**, citing the book *Women Don't Ask* by Linda Babcock and Sara Laschever. Women are less likely to start a negotiation, and they feel more uncomfortable about negotiation. They tend to expect less and get less. Women are less likely to negotiate their first salary, which costs them a lot of money in the long run. But women who consistently negotiate their (first salary and) raises earn a lot more than do other women over the course of a career... so, *man up*, ladies!

Preparation is absolutely crucial in negotiation. That includes research on the specifics of the negotiation, but it also includes mental preparation. Now, let's take a look at how to avoid getting lied to in a negotiation.

Four steps to a lie-proof negotiation:

One: Upgrade your negotiation philosophy: Some take an adversarial, **win-lose** approach to negotiating - you are working *against* the other negotiator - but research shows that negotiators are more likely to lie in this type of negotiation. The alternative is a **win-win** negotiation, in which the parties work *together* to figure out which concessions can be made by each side without anyone going home unhappy. The author recommends for you to set the tone and try to direct the negotiation toward win-win.

Sounds keen. So, what are some win-win tactics?

Set your limits: To misrepresent facts is illegal, but **"puffing"** up the truth through exaggerated statements of opinion and praise for your product, or the quality of the deal which you're offering, is not illegal; nevertheless, you should set a limit on exactly how far you will go with your puffing.

Avoid false promises: Research shows that making false promises is damaging to negotiators in the long run.

Declare your honest ways: This will make it more likely that the other party will relax a bit and not lie to you.

Two: Prepare, prepare, prepare: First off, make sure the deal is a good enough fit between you and the other party so as to make it worth your time. If it is a good fit, then try to negotiate with the other side's final decision maker.

In addition to deciding on your bottom line and a list of deal breakers, make a list of points that need to be discussed during the negotiation. Also, decide which specific concessions are doable.

Prepare to ask the specific questions that will get you the missing data that you need to know. Of course, also prepare to answer the same types of questions on your end (and be ready for all kinds of questions), and have your data printed out or ready to be transferred.

Three: Take control of the setting, the ground rules, and the conversation: Demand a face-to-face meeting, which will give you a chance to read (and to communicate better with) the other negotiator. If you can choose the meeting place, select a warm and friendly environment, which promotes openness. And try to sit in a way that allows you to see as much of the other negotiator as possible, including his legs, which speak volumes when they shake (indicative of nervousness, and possibly deception).

Once you've formed a rapport with the other negotiator (perhaps before the main negotiation), suggest that each of you brings in a witness to watch the negotiation, which can promote honesty.

Clearly articulate the issues to avoid confusion (or feigned confusion) that could lead to last minute requests for changes.

Draft a confidentiality agreement that outlines who is privy to the information that is revealed during the negotiation.

Four: Lie-proof the close: It is not a lie to frame the outcome as a gain. For example, if a buyer offered 80% of the asking price and wound up paying 90% of the ask, frame the outcome as a 10% discount off of the asking price and give him a pat on the tush. This could help your relationship going forward. Speaking of which, when you can foresee a long-term relationship with the other party, mention it; this will make it harder for the other negotiator to lie to you.

Before wrapping up the negotiation, ask a "catch-all" question, such as, "What haven't we discussed that is important for me to know about?"

After the negotiation, review your notes regarding the tentatively agreed upon deal, and then have the other party confirm them via email, so that there is a record.

Job applications: This is an important negotiation, and perhaps that's why so many resumes are fictitious. One study found that 44% of resumes contain fabrications, and another study found that 83% of undergrads had lied to get a job.

In addition to the desperation that some job markets cause and the general pressure to land a job, another reason that applicants lie is because they assume that companies are not trustworthy and will lie to *them*. Similarly, ageism might make an older applicant fear that he won't get a fair shake, which he might use as a justification for lying about his age. Other types of bias (or perceived bias) in workplaces might lead to similar results.

Sometimes, an applicant will lie to get his foot in the door, and then he'll have to keep lying later on.

So, watch out for all of these, and sharpen your detection skills by reviewing the first half of the book.

CHAPTER 8: The Deception Audit

A deception audit is a service provided by auditors who will come in and examine all the areas in which your business and workplace are susceptible to deception. Afterward, you should be able to use the information and tools that you've acquired to improve honesty among your ranks, and doing so can lead to stronger long-term financial performance and all sorts of benefits.

Who needs a deception audit?

Scenario 1: Crisis management: Even once a crisis has developed, it's not too late for an audit, which can actually be the first step toward fixing the problem.

Scenario 2: Confronting organizational change: A sweeping change in strategy or a merger with another company can breed confusion, fear, and resentment, bringing trust to a low, and the potential for deception to a high. A deception audit can help in the transition.

Scenario 3: Testing the health of your company or team: The best time to run an audit is *now*, preventatively, *before* you run into any problems.

The three phases of a deception audit:

Phase 1: Data collection: Questionnaires, assessments, and thorough interviews of key managers.

Phase 2: Corporate incentive structure mapping: Identifies structural flaws and bad practices in a company that can inadvertently create paths to deceit.

Phase 3: Committing to change: It's a long-term process. Don't bother to bring in an expert if you're not committed to seeing the process through.

CHAPTER 9: Building Your Brain Trust

One way to combat lies in business is to surround yourself with a core group of people whom you trust. Start with the network of people with whom you've already had an association. Identify those who fit specific roles, and make sure that they are up-to-date in their knowledge of the relevant fields in which they are expected to lend their expertise.

Before inviting anyone into your brain trust, examine the trajectory of the your relationship with him. Has your relationship headed in a direction that makes him less than the ideal candidate? Has he changed over time? Can he remain both loyal and objective?

Once you've picked the best candidates from your network, identify what is still needed to round out the team. You will need business associates and paid advisers, but also make sure to include some forward thinkers. Meet candidates face-to-face, and be clear in your expectations.

Good luck!

Thanks for reading, you busy human!

Please leave a review... if you're not too busy.

:)

Printed in Great Britain
by Amazon

69665433R00020